MW01196077

RETIRE AND THRIVE

THE 7 LESSONS THAT WILL HELP YOU EMBRACE YOUR NEXT CHAPTER WITH PURPOSE, WEALTH, AND CONFIDENCE

DAN LANGWORTHY

ethos
collective

Retire and Thrive

© 2024 by Dan Langworthy

www.fortressfg.net

Published by Ethos Collective
Powell, OH
EthosCollective.vip

Library of Congress Cataloging Number: 2024909210
Paperback ISBN: 978-1-63680-289-3
Hardback ISBN: 978-1-63680-290-9
eBook ISBN: 978-1-63680-291-6

Information contained herein was accurate at the time of first publication. Please consult a financial specialist to ensure you have the most up-to-date information.

Dedicated to and in memory of
Merece Langworthy.
I'm grateful for the blessing of a mother
who taught me the importance
of enriching the lives of others.

Table of Contents

Foreword ix
Note to the Reader xiii

Part One: Parable

Retirement: Blessing or Burden 3
Scott and Donna's Story 7
    Life Before Children 8
    Children Change Everything 10

Part Two: Paradigm

Lesson One: I Can Enjoy the Fruits of My Labor 17
    Empty Nest 19
    Enjoying the Fruits of Your Labor 21

Lesson Two: To Reap the Rewards,
I Must Review My Investments 23
    Portfolio Reviews 24
    Understanding Stocks. 27

Lesson Three: I Only Have Freedom
When My Cash Flows Freely 29
    A Debt Free Retirement Plan. 31
    If You Have Debt, Make Sure It's Smart Debt. 32

Lesson Four: I Will Thrive
As I Understand My Financial Picture 35
    Taking Inventory of Your Assets. 36
    Thriving for the Rest of Your Life 38

Lesson Five: I Must Navigate Social Security
with Wisdom 41
    Word of Wisdom One: Timing 42
    Word of Wisdom Two: Taxes. 44
    Word of Wisdom Three: Spousal Benefits. 45
    Word of Wisdom Four: Survivor Benefits 46

Lesson Six: I Can Make Taxes Work for Me
Instead of Against Me 47
    How Much Have You Borrowed
    from Your Rich Uncle. 48
    Filling Your Buckets. 49

Lesson Seven: To Have a Bigger Future,
I Must Make Today Matter 52
    Prepare for Impact 54
    Win the Fight 56

One Year Later. 58
    The Best Laid Plans. 59

A Bigger Future 60
Back in Minnesota 63

Part Three: Pathways

Next Steps 67
Find Meaning and Purpose 68
What Do I Look for in a Financial Advisor? 69

Further Resources 71
Key Takeaways 73
Part One: Parable 73
Part Two: Paradigm 73
Part Three: Pathways 75
About the Author 77

Foreword

As I sit down to write this foreword for *Retire and Thrive: The 7 Lessons that Will Help You Embrace Your Next Chapter with Purpose, Wealth, and Confidence,* I am reminded of one profound truth: retirement isn't just about reaching a certain age and stepping away from the workforce; it's about embarking on a new journey filled with purpose, wealth, and confidence. This new and powerful parable by Dan Langworthy will drive that home for you in a fun and educational way.

In our fast-paced world, the concept of retirement has evolved. No longer is it solely about leisurely days spent on a porch swing, but rather, it's about harnessing the fruits of one's labor and navigating the financial landscape with wisdom and foresight. It's about leveraging one's resources to create a fulfilling and abundant life post-career. And in *Retire and Thrive,* Dan Langworthy masterfully unpacks the seven essential lessons that will guide you towards a retirement filled with vitality and prosperity.

Lesson 1: I Can Enjoy the Fruits of My Labor

Dan begins by instilling a crucial mindset shift: that you deserve to enjoy the fruits of your labor. After years of hard work and dedication, it's time to reap the rewards and savor the joys that retirement brings. Dan empowers readers to embrace this newfound freedom and live life to the fullest.

Lesson 2: To Reap the Rewards, I Must Review My Investments

Investing wisely is paramount to a thriving retirement, and Dan delves into the importance of reviewing and optimizing your investment portfolio. With a keen understanding of financial markets and investment strategies, he equips readers with the tools they need to maximize their returns and secure their financial future.

Lesson 3: I Only Have Freedom When My Cash Flows Freely

True freedom in retirement is contingent upon healthy cash flow management. Dan emphasizes the significance of maintaining a steady stream of income to support your desired lifestyle. By cultivating a mindset of abundance and implementing sound financial practices, readers can attain the financial freedom they crave.

Lesson 4: I Will Thrive as I Understand My Financial Picture

Understanding your financial landscape is key to making informed decisions and achieving financial success. Dan guides readers through the process of assessing their financial situation, identifying areas for improvement, and creating a roadmap for long-term prosperity. With clarity comes confidence, and Dan empowers readers to take control of their financial destinies.

Lesson 5: I Must Navigate Social Security with Wisdom

Navigating the complexities of Social Security can be daunting, but Dan breaks down the intricacies in a clear and accessible manner. From maximizing benefits to optimizing timing, he provides invaluable guidance to help readers make the most of this essential retirement resource.

Lesson 6: I Can Make Taxes Work for Me Instead of Against Me

Taxes are an inevitable part of life, but they need not be a burden in retirement. Dan demonstrates how strategic tax planning can minimize liabilities and maximize savings, allowing readers to keep more of their hard-earned money in their pockets. By leveraging tax-efficient strategies, readers can enhance their financial well-being and build wealth for generations to come.

Lesson 7: To Have a Bigger Future, I Must Make Today Matter

Finally, Dan underscores the importance of seizing the present moment and taking proactive steps towards a brighter future. Retirement isn't just about planning for tomorrow;

it's about living with intention today. By prioritizing purpose and embracing opportunity, readers can cultivate a fulfilling retirement that surpasses their wildest dreams.

In *Retire and Thrive*, Dan Langworthy has crafted a comprehensive roadmap for navigating the complexities of retirement with confidence and clarity. His wisdom, gleaned from years of experience in the financial industry, shines through on every page, offering readers invaluable insights and actionable advice. Whether you're nearing retirement age or just beginning to plan for the future, this book is an indispensable resource for anyone seeking to retire with purpose, wealth, and confidence.

As you embark on this transformative journey towards retirement, may Dan's teachings serve as your guiding light, illuminating the path to a life of abundance and fulfillment. May you retire not just gracefully, but triumphantly, embracing your next chapter with open arms and boundless optimism.

Here's to your prosperous retirement,
Chris Widener
Best Selling Author of The Art of Influence
ChrisWidener.com

Note to the Reader

For the past thirty-five years, I've been helping people navigate the retirement maze. As I've watched clients enter and leave my office, I've asked myself, What is the difference between the people I meet who are living a successful retirement–joyful, fulfilled, and excited to get up everyday–and those who feel alone and lost? What is the secret to living an abundant retirement? Recently, I've felt the answer is in how we respond to the seven lessons you'll find in this book.

I enjoy helping people prepare for their "go-go" years–that time between ages sixty and seventy-five when we can reap the rewards of our hard work. I especially love it when we can begin planning early. However, many wait until they turn fifty to start seriously thinking about life after their day job. While it's obviously easier to set yourself up to live your dreams when you look into your future at age thirty, it's never too late to create a plan for your future.

The parable you're about to encounter is fictional. Nevertheless, the lessons Scott shares with Blake are very real. Their stories are built from the countless clients I've assisted as they've moved toward retirement. In fact, their stories could be your story.

Nearly every retiree struggles with at least a few of these aspects as they step into the final third of their time on planet Earth. My goal is to help you understand and prepare for the nuances of life after sixty. Hopefully, you'll resonate with Scott and Blake, and their stories will empower you to embrace the next chapter of your life with purpose, wealth, and confidence. May each of the lessons you learn in these pages allow you to live life to the fullest—to *Retire and Thrive*.

PART ONE

Parable

You are never too old to set a new goal or dream a new dream.

—*C.S. Lewis*

Retirement: Blessing or Burden

An Investment in Knowledge Pays the Best Interest.
—Benjamin Franklin

The first drop of rain fell as Scott hit the button to lower the hatch on his SUV. We finished that round of golf just in time. Driving home, he mulled over his conversation with Blake during those last nine holes—especially those last few moments as they retrieved their clubs from the cart.

• • •

"You mean you don't check your investment accounts at least a couple of times every week?" Blake had asked.

"No, we feel pretty secure." Scott answered.

"The closer Mary and I get to retirement, the more I worry about what the market will do to our future."

"I used to stress over that, but Donna and I ended up structuring our retirement accounts so those huge ups and downs have less impact."

"I think I need to pick your brain then, because I'm losing sleep thinking about where we're going to be financially when Mary and I retire next year. Maybe you and I could meet for coffee Saturday morning."

"Not this Saturday. My grandson, Ethan, is flying in to visit. He's got a long weekend because of the holiday on Monday. Let's plan on lunch at my place after men's league next week," Scott offered.

"Sounds perfect," Blake said as he wiped the grass stain off his last club.

• • •

Scott had retired a little over a year ago, but he and Donna began planning for life beyond their day jobs five years earlier. They never dreamed they'd be able to afford a second home, but as soon as that idea became a reality, they started the search. They knew they wanted to spend winters someplace warmer than their Minnesota homeland, and they needed a place big enough to house their children and grandchildren for a week or two at a time. With friends in Fort Myers and Arizona, a brother in New Mexico, and Donna's college roommate in Houston, they had plenty of friend-filled options.

Three years, six vacations, and a dozen friends later, they knew Scottsdale would be their winter home. The sun, low humidity, and magnificent golf courses caught their attention, but downtown Scottsdale with all its shops and restaurants, as well as its proximity to the airport, clinched the location.

Blake and Mary were among those Arizona friends Scott and Donna had visited during their search. Scott and Blake had worked together for fifteen years before Blake found this new job in Phoenix almost twenty years ago. Though they'd stayed in touch and visited back and forth a few times, it was good to spend time with his friend two or three times a week again.

Blake's questions about retirement reminded Scott of his own worries before he and Donna decided to retire. For most of their lives, they'd imagined enduring the cold northern winters. Both had spent their entire lives in the snow belt. Their parents and grandparents had endured the frigid seasons just fine. They assumed they could too.

• • •

"I'm back," Scott announced as he walked through the door.

He heard his wife's muffled call from the backyard. "How was your game?"

"Better than last week." Scott laughed as he headed toward the sliding glass doors off the great room. "But Blake asked me some questions about our retirement, and he got me to thinking about where we were ten years ago."

"You mean before we met Julianne?"

"Exactly."

"I feel like I need to put a coat on to even consider it. Have you seen the Minnesota weather report for February? If we hadn't listened to her, we'd be facing a blizzard today instead of getting in the pool."

Scott laughed. "Blake checks his investment accounts several times a week. He wants me to tell him our secret next week after golf."

"I remember how miserable you were looking at those numbers that often," Donna said as Scott settled into the chair next to her.

"My worrying about it nearly sent you to a divorce attorney." The atmosphere grew a little solemn as the two remembered those rough years.

"You spent every moment either working or focusing on how to manage our funds so we wouldn't go broke. I felt like we weren't even a couple. Do you think Blake's wife is having the same struggle?"

"He didn't say. But I can tell he's stressing at least as much as I did."

Scott and Donna's Story

You cannot make progress without making decisions.

—Jim Rohn

Scott and Donna's three children all still lived in their hometown in Minnesota. While their younger four grandchildren still lived with their parents, the oldest three attended colleges across the country. Though Scott and Donna spent a good deal of time with their family all summer, those oldest grandchildren had jobs and internships—not to mention friends who lived across the country, so time with them had become more precious. After they moved to Scottsdale, the grandparents decided to gift them round-trip plane tickets to Arizona for their birthdays each year, and Ethan was cashing in his gift this weekend.

Ethan's flight landed just in time for dinner on Friday. Since Donna's creative arts class was sponsoring a special event, Scott met his grandson's plane.

On the way into town, Ethan, a senior at Ball State, told Scott about the internship he had participated in. "It looks like it could turn into a full-time job in June, Pap. They have a few openings in architect design."

Listening to Ethan's excitement, Scott couldn't help but think about his conversation with Blake. How might things be different if someone had talked to them about retirement right after they graduated from college?

Grandfather and grandson grabbed sandwiches at a café and sat at an outdoor table nearby. "Does this firm have any benefits, Ethan?"

"Yeah, I haven't heard all the details, but I know there's some sort of healthcare and a 401(k). I'm really not sure exactly what I should be looking for in benefits. Do you think I'm too young to worry about that? Maybe I should just be grateful I have a decent job."

"I guess it depends on where you see yourself in forty years."

"Wow. Forty years . . . I'm not sure where I see myself in two. But watching you and Grandma have fun here in Arizona all winter makes me wonder if I could do something like this someday."

"Would you like to know some of the secrets your grandmother and I have learned over the years?"

"I'm all ears."

Life Before Children

So, Scott started. "How did you like working at the grocery store your last two years of high school, Ethan?"

"It was okay, I guess. It wasn't a hard job. It was cool to finally not have to ask mom for gas money."

"How much did you save?"

"Dad made me open a savings account and told me since he gave me a car to drive and paid for my cell phone and car insurance, I had to save half of every paycheck."

Scott chuckled. "Okay. Well, how much would you have saved if your dad hadn't made you?"

"Well, since I completely blew the other half and wished I could use the rest for a spring break getaway and buying gadgets for my car . . ." Ethan paused and let out a quiet sigh. "I guess I wouldn't have been very responsible with it."

"Hey, I didn't ask to make you feel bad about it. That's how most of us are when we're seventeen. But you're twenty-two now. That's just two years younger than I was when I met your grandmother. I didn't save much while I was in high school either. And when I got my first job out of college, I didn't do much better. I loved the freedom of having my own money. But I made so much more than I did in high school, my savings account grew even though I wasn't very intentional about saving. To be honest, retirement didn't even cross my mind. I sometimes wonder how much I would have if I'd put more thought into it."

Scott could tell he had spurred Ethan to do some thinking. He paused long enough to take a few bites of his sandwich then continued, "Fortunately, my employer offered a matching 401(k), so I started contributing five percent to take advantage of the match. After about a year, the investment company's representative told me increasing my 401(k) contributions would give me a comfortable retirement. I had just met Grandma and still lived with your great-grandparents, so I upped my contribution to fifteen percent of my paycheck.

With the company's match at five percent, I stashed away twenty percent of my pay for several years."

Scott stopped for a moment to give his grandson time to digest everything he'd said. He could see the wheels turning. Ethan was impressed. "If I put twenty percent a year in a 401(k) for forty years . . . And interest . . ." He paused as he tried to do the math in his head.

"When you're young with almost no expenses it adds up fast." Scott chuckled. "But we didn't put twenty percent in for forty years."

Children Change Everything

"What happened?" Ethan asked.

"Your dad!" Scott laughed.

As they finished their dinner, Scott gave Ethan the highlights of his first few years of marriage and how having children modified their financial situation. He told his grandson about the many life changes he and Donna experienced between the ages of twenty-six and forty-five. Each variation meant their investment portfolio looked a little different.

Donna worked as a designer, and Scott loved his job as a purchasing manager. They moved from an apartment into a small house when they decided to grow their family. And when their first son, James, arrived, Scott and Donna both dropped their 401(k) contributions to five percent. They wanted to make sure they took advantage of everything their employers would match, but they needed more in their pocket to cover the cost of a child and a house.

The birth of Madison a year later invited a discussion on childcare. Donna had hated missing so many of James' firsts, and her parents weren't physically able to run after two toddlers. With the cost of daycare to consider and the fact she and Scott both believed the kids would benefit from a stay-at-home mom, Donna put in her resignation. With only a passing thought about retirement, and sixty-five feeling very far away, they eliminated Donna's salary and reduced Scott's 401(k) contribution.

Scott and his grandson sat there for almost an hour as he told Ethan about his layoff just after his Aunt Madison was born. The six months of unemployment brought them close to the breaking point.

The young man's jaw dropped when he found out they almost lost his grandmother after she gave birth to her third child. Scott had to back off his 401(k) for about six months to pay for Donna's extended hospital stay after Noah came. Later, they found themselves nearly wiped out when Donna had breast cancer at age thirty. Even with health insurance, the medical bills took a chunk of their savings.

"We had so many unexpected expenses and setbacks during those first twenty years, but now we're grateful we added so much to our 401(k)s when we didn't know any better. And Grandma and I want to make sure you, your siblings, and your cousins learn from our life."

Ethan was amazed. "What would you two be doing if you and Grandma had kept up like you did before you had kids? What you have now seems awesome. But it sounds like you're telling me you could have more. You guys could have traveled the world for the rest of your lives. That's crazy!"

"Grandma and I don't have any misgivings about our decision for her to stay at home with your dad and aunt and uncle. We feel like her being with them was worth more than any money we might have right now. And we feel blessed to have made it through the tough times so well. We even set up college funds for all three kids. Every time one of them turned two, we opened an account. We could have grown our 401(k)s even more if we hadn't put aside that extra six hundred dollars every month, but we wanted to make sure they could get a degree without debt if they wanted to."

"It never dawned on me that my last four years cut into dad and mom's retirement," Ethan said softly.

"You shouldn't feel bad about that. We didn't regret one penny we saved for our kids, and I know your parents don't either. But I never thought to talk to your dad about preparing for retirement, and I wish I had. There's so much I didn't think about at your age."

Scott had come to understand every life decision impacted his retirement picture, and he wanted his grandchildren to face life's changes armed with information. He felt like he and Donna got lucky. Despite the fact they could have used the wisdom Julianne gave them years earlier, most of the choices they made—even the ones that cut into their retirement investments—ended well.

"I don't want to tell you how to spend your money, Ethan. It's just that since I moved into my sixties, I've come to realize much of our comfortable life came because we were disciplined in our thirties and forties. We made a plan and stuck with it. That consistency gave us our winter home in Arizona. Grandma and I just want you to be aware that every choice you make matters, and it's never too early to start thinking about what you want to do when you're our age—even if the plan changes a dozen times before you get there. I know you still feel like a kid, but looking back, I wish I had found a financial advisor when I started my first 401(k)."

"Maybe I should talk to your guy when I get home this summer."

"Or girl . . . Julianne helped us more than we ever imagined. Grandma and I would love to introduce you to the firm we work with."

"Thanks, Pap." The two stood and hugged.

"OK, enough heavy talk. Let's get to the house. Grandma will have ice cream on the back porch waiting for you. So, what do you want to do while you're here?"

• • •

Life hits everyone hard. Regardless of how well we plan, things we never imagined come at us. Scott and Donna went through several seasons that beat them down. In fact, when a heavy snowfall caused the garage roof to cave in and Scott faced a second layoff just as Donna finished her last round of chemo, they thought they might have to file bankruptcy. They had watched two of their friends start over from scratch after losing their house and both cars. Fortunately, the layoff ended earlier than anticipated, and with a little downsizing on some of their other expenses, they squeaked through.

In addition to their unique hurdles, the couple faced financial burdens almost everyone will encounter. Helping care for their parents, raising children through broken bones and a couple crashed cars, as well as partially funding college took their toll. Maybe you've felt like this Minnesota couple. By the time they were fifty, they worried they might never retire. But after they learned the seven great lessons for retirement, everything changed.

PART TWO

Paradigm

We must all suffer from one of two pains: the pain of discipline or the pain of regret. The difference is discipline weighs ounces while regret weighs tons.

—Jim Rohn

LESSON ONE

I Can Enjoy the Fruits of My Labor

Success in investing doesn't correlate with IQ ...
what you need is the temperament to control the urges
that get other people into trouble in investing.

—*Warren Buffett*

The few days between Ethan's departure and Scott's weekly golf league passed quickly. "How did you manage that drive on seven?" Scott asked Blake as they settled into the chairs on the back patio. "I've never seen you hit one that far."

"I got a hold of the ball just right for a change."

After fifteen minutes of small talk and downing the salads they picked up on the way back from the course, Blake took them to the purpose of their lunch. "Alright. I want to know the secret. How do you keep from worrying about the volatility of the market? I know the way I'm stressing over it isn't good for me."

"I actually owe my peace of mind to a few lessons I've learned over the years and some valuable information we got from a financial advisor named Julianne," Scott replied. "To be honest, we also owe some of where we are now to difficulties we faced along the way.

"I know you can't go back and redo the last thirty years, but a good part of our current situation is due to the fact we put as much as we could in our 401(k)s year after year. We sacrificed vacations and kept our cars simple through the years. At one point after Noah was born, we talked about getting a bigger house, but we decided the boys could share a room. Julianne calls it our accumulation years."

"Mary and I have been adding to our accounts since we graduated. But we've had some setbacks. Do you remember when our middle son got thrown from that horse? We both ended up needing more time off than we had accrued in paid leave. At the time we felt grateful both our companies were gracious and flexible during the surgeries, doctor's appointments, and hospital stays. But since we had chosen a larger medical deductible to save on our premiums, the bills took their toll. That was just one of the seasons when we couldn't even put in the matching amount into our 401(k)."

"We had the same issues when Donna had cancer and I had layoffs. But when Julianne looked at everything we had put in over the years, she showed us that we had more than enough to live comfortably in retirement. And you had Mary adding to her 401(k) all those years, too."

"So, you think we'll be better off than I imagine?"

"You'll need to talk to a financial advisor to get the full picture, but I'm guessing you shouldn't be any worse off than Donna and me."

"I wish I could stop worrying. I really admire how you don't seem to give your retirement accounts a second thought."

Empty Nest

"Much of our mental freedom as well as the extra we have to get the grandkids here once a year came because of changes we made in our investment accounts during our empty nest years."

"Did you and Donna have trouble reconnecting after your kids moved out? Mary has been worried that we've just delayed our empty nest syndrome because she's been working so much. I'm pretty sure we'll be fine, but I feel bad just dismissing what she says."

"Donna and I attended two couples' retreats while the kids were in high school. They said many couples have a hard time connecting with one another after their children leave home. Often one spouse focuses so heavily on their teenagers' activities they lose their own identity and don't know their husband or wife when the last child graduates. In other situations, the main breadwinner spends their children's high school years plunging themselves into work. Even those who set up college funds early start to feel the pressure, and the parents who didn't might feel overwhelmed.

"Donna and I feel like we avoided some of that because we saved for the three kids' college funds and raised our children according to that proverb, 'Train up a child in the way he should go, and when he is old, he will not depart from it.'[1] We raised James, Madison, and Noah with the belief our ultimate responsibility was to deliver responsible and productive adults to the world. Rather than feeling abandoned or like she had nothing left to give, Donna felt free. She went back to work for a few years and took up golf. And I felt satisfied knowing our three kids were so successful."

---

[1]   Proverbs 22:6 KJV

"Mary and I feel pretty good about our kids, too. I'm actually more concerned about after we both quit working. We've focused on little else since our daughters graduated. Mary loves her job, but as the Executive Assistant to the VP of the company, she gets called for ridiculous things night and day. I wonder if she'll feel lost when that's not consuming her time."

"Being separated by jobs is the other thing they warned us about at the couples' retreats." Scott paused for a moment, "Do you and Mary still date?"

"What do you mean? We've moved past dating forty years ago. See the ring?"

Scott grinned. "If you want to make sure you don't have problems connecting after you both quit working, you need to call Mary on your way home a few times a month and ask her out. Go do something fun together, and if you really want to impress her, you plan it. Don't ask her what she wants to do."

"You do that?"

"You bet. We took all the advice we got at those retreats to heart, and it has really worked for us. It also gave us more intentional time to have those discussions about retirement."

Scott continued, "We always talked about me retiring no later than my sixty-fifth birthday. But we didn't get serious about the discussions until after Noah graduated. That meant we had less than ten years to prepare. That's about the time I started looking for a financial advisor to get the best help possible. I interviewed three others before I met Julianne. She adjusted some of our funds, helped us take advantage of the tax laws for 401(k)s, and advised us to make the most of our last decade before retirement."

● ● ●

The empty nest years give everyone in the workforce a final opportunity to build retirement funds. Though many variables affect contributions—things Scott learned in other lessons—this last push for a comfortable and thriving retirement lifestyle gave this Minnesota/Scottsdale couple a bit of motivation as they finished the career phase of their life.

Enjoying the Fruits of Your Labor

"One of the first things Julianne told us when we went in to set up our retirement disbursements was that we needed to think of these years as a reward for a lifetime of hard work. She told us to take to heart that famous phrase, 'Eat, drink, and enjoy the fruits of your labor.'[2] I'm not sure why we felt like we needed permission to spend our own money, but her words helped us look at our financial picture and buy this house in Scottsdale. Before we met her, we worried about how much we would leave our children when we were gone. But Julianne showed us that we raised our children well. They have great jobs and don't need our money. If we have a bit left over for them to inherit, it will be a nice bonus. But now that we've moved past our accumulation phase, it's time to reap the reward of all our hard work. Julianne calls it the distribution phase.

"On top of that, she worked with us to make our funds less dependent on the market now that we're retired. Have you and Mary made a list of things you want to do after you have more time?"

"With Mary working so many hours and me stressing over the money we'll have, neither of us have thought much

---

[2]   Ecclesiastes 3:13 TLB

about how we'll use the funds I'm all worked up about. That's pretty sad, isn't it?"

"There you go! Something to talk about during date night. Julianne gave us that homework ten years ago. She used the list to advise us and adjust our investments so we would be financially free to live that list."

A notification tone interrupted the conversation.

"Sorry, I have to run," Blake said as he stood and held up his phone. "It's work."

"I thought you had Thursdays off since they hired that new guy to transition into your spot after you retire next year."

"Yeah, but the text said the plant had a major shut down. They need supplies to recover by tomorrow. I haven't introduced the new guy to all my emergency connections yet. I guess today's the day."

Scott stood and laughed. "No one except the plant supervisor knows that the purchasing manager is the real hero."

"Let me grab my cape." Blake headed for the door. "Can we finish this conversation this evening?"

"Sure, why don't you bring Mary so the ladies can visit?"

"She'll enjoy the break. I'll see you then."

LESSON TWO

To Reap the Rewards, I Must Review My Investments

It's not how much money you make,
but how much money you keep,
how hard it works for you,
and how many generations you keep it for.

—*Robert Kiyosaki*

The aroma of fresh-baked cookies greeted Blake and Mary when Donna opened the door.

"Oh, I hope that smell is for us," Blake said.

"Absolutely! Come on in. Scott is already out by the pool."

"Thanks so much for taking time to help us with this," Mary told her friend as she gave Donna a hug.

"We live so close, and these guys see each other every week. How is it you and I haven't visited in a month?" Donna replied.

"I work at least forty hours in the office and ten more at home every week. I don't have time to do anything. Even though I love my job, I can't wait until retirement."

"And that's why we need this conversation. We have to give this beautiful lady some time off."

Donna picked up the tray of cookies and led Blake and Mary to the back patio where Scott waited with four cups—two full of iced tea and the other two with lemonade.

Portfolio Reviews

Scott poured the evening refreshments while Blake got the conversation started.

"Mary and I have been talking about this idea of living in the accumulation phase and then moving into the distribution phase, but I'm worried. What if we haven't accumulated enough?"

"Blake, when was the last time you met with a financial advisor?"

"I meet with the guy the company brings in every year."

"I used to do that, too. My first manager told me, 'You're young, so invest big.' And I did. But by the time I turned forty, my portfolio had grown to the point I started worrying about it all being in the market. I played that game you've been dabbling in—constantly worrying about my money."

"He almost lost me during those years," Donna chimed in. "I felt like he was obsessed, and I was just an accessory—almost a burden."

"I'm glad I'm not the only one who ever felt like that." Mary shared.

"Wait. You feel like you're a burden?" Blake was genuinely surprised.

"Blake, until you talked to Scott last week, you've never said a word to me about what's been troubling you. I knew you were on your computer all the time, but I had no idea you were obsessing over the market. For all I knew you were on a dating site."

"Exactly!" Donna brought laughter to the table.

Scott continued, "So after the last big market drop—and discovering Donna had considered calling an attorney—I started to talk to her about my worries. We had worked so hard to grow our 401(k)s. After so many sacrifices, I couldn't bear to let them sink. Colleagues told me not to worry because I had at least ten to fifteen years before retirement. But that just sat like a pit in my stomach. Confiding in Donna what was going on in my brain was one of the best decisions I made. She's the one who suggested we find a good advisor."

"Julianne had nearly twenty years of experience specializing in retirement planning when we met her," Donna interjected. "She shared multiple stories of how she'd seen the stock market drop drastically, but every time, it rebounded to the previous high and eventually even higher. It can take as little as six months to come back, but on a few occasions, it took years. Fortunately, we weren't planning to retire for at least another decade, so she believed we would be fine. She definitely helped put Scott's mind at ease."

"And she informed me my investments looked like I was in my twenties despite the fact I'd recently turned fifty-five."

Blake was shocked. "Age makes a difference?"

"That's the same question I asked Julianne. She informed us that by age fifty-five, since retirement was on the horizon, we needed to have a smaller percentage of our portfolio in more aggressive investments. We hadn't moved anything in our portfolio since I talked to the guy from the 401(k) place when I was in my thirties. And since I wasn't going to need anything out of it for at least thirty years, it made sense to choose the high-risk, high-return option. Everything has time to rebound when you're that far from the retirement window. The market was still pretty volatile when we met with Julianne, so some of our investments were facing huge fluctuations."

Donna finished for Scott. "Shortly after the market recovered—just like Julianne said it would—she helped us diversify our portfolio to make it more conservative based on our age. Now it produces a bit lower return, but it's more protected from market downturns."

"Now we meet with someone from the firm every year to make sure everything still fits with our plans." Scott sounded excited as he continued. "And the best part—ever since we started doing the annual review, I don't feel like I have to check the portfolio every few days. It's like Julianne set me free."

Mary joined the conversation. "We might need to get Julianne's phone number."

"She retired about the same time Scott did," Donna said.

"But she left us in good hands," Scott pointed out. "And before she retired, she helped us understand the importance of scoping out our next horizon."

Scott saw the look of confusion before Blake said a word. "Every year before we meet with Julianne's replacement, Samantha, Donna and I make a list of things we think we'll need or want to do in the next eighteen months. We talk about vacations, appliances, cars. . ."

Donna interrupted, "And the number of grandkids that will need plane tickets the next year."

Scott laughed. "Exactly. Any large expenses we might see on the horizon. Then we decide which of those we might need to finance with extra withdrawals from our portfolio. Samantha makes sure any money we'll need during the next twelve to eighteen months is invested in safe, secure short-term investments. We're fortunate to have enough that some of our portfolio, a portion we can let sit and grow for more years, is giving us a larger return because it's in investments that have a bigger fluctuation."

"We definitely need that phone number," Mary said.

"You probably could find someone right here in Scottsdale." Donna was always so practical.

Blake read Mary's mind. "Mary doesn't have the free time to help me find someone we trust. It would make sense for us to get in touch with a team you've already vetted."

"I'll get you their number before you leave," Donna promised.

Understanding Stocks

By the time they finished their conversation, the late winter sun had completely dropped below the horizon. And even though the week had been unseasonably warm, the coolness of evening had swept in. The four talked about their children and grandchildren and made plans to go to the Grand Canyon together before Scott and Donna headed back to Minnesota for the summer. However, before they left the subject of retirement and finances, Scott expanded a bit on what they learned about the rise and fall of stocks.

As Julianne helped Scott and Donna get ready for retirement, she moved their portfolio into more conservative areas. She added stocks that paid dividends as well as bonds. She also explained that when it came to stocks, they needed to think of themselves as business owners. Every stock in their portfolio meant they indirectly owned a piece of that company. Regardless of the dips in the market, as long as that business didn't completely close, they could not lose all their money—something that scared some of their friends. After Julianne told them how it worked, Scott started to feel bad for friends who had sold investments out of fear as soon as the prices began to drop. He and Donna had seen many of those same market numbers rise even higher than before the dip. They ended up with a greater return on some of those risky investments; however, they knew friends had lost money by selling low.

As the famous investor Warren Buffet says, "Concentration builds wealth, diversification protects wealth." Remembering those rough seasons as they shared with Blake and Mary made Scott and Donna once again grateful they had found Julianne and her firm when they did. Their annual reviews helped them avoid the stress Blake currently felt, and the knowledge Julianne had given them gave them confidence and peace of mind as they reaped the rewards of the sacrifices they made throughout the years.

Mary thought she saw some relief on her husband's face when they stood to leave a few hours later. "I'm so glad you and Blake started this conversation. I was starting to think I would never be able to retire."

Blake reached out to shake Scott's hand. "So, when can you give me your next piece of advice?"

"How 'bout a lesson and a pickleball match on Saturday?"

"I'll be there."

LESSON THREE

I Only Have Freedom
When My Cash Flows Freely

*Making more money will not solve your problems
if cash flow management is your problem.*

—*Robert Kiyosaki*

Blake and Scott met at the courts about an hour earlier than their ten a.m. reservation. They grabbed coffee and relaxed at one of the tables on the patio near the action.

"I'm glad I'm not going up against one of those guys," Scott told Blake as they watched two other retirees battle it out.

"You know it," Blake replied. "Okay, we only have an hour. So, what else do I need to know before I retire next year?"

"Do you remember I told you some of the lessons we learned came through our difficulties? Back when Donna was going through her chemo treatments and I faced those layoffs, we both had brand-new, high-end cars. The payments we had at the time nearly took us under. We ended up selling Donna's car for less than it was worth just to get out from under the payments. That's when we learned we either had to control our debt or our debt would control us.

"When Donna and I started to talk about retirement, we agreed controlling debt would be doubly important. I don't want Donna to struggle like my mom did after Dad died. He worked until he was seventy, but they had refinanced the house to do some major repairs just a few years before he retired. They used Mom's entire social security check to pay the mortgage every month. It didn't seem like a big deal. They could easily live on Dad's check and his retirement. But when we lost Dad at seventy-two, Mom still had eight years on the loan. She lost one-third of their combined income every month, so she had to get two jobs to cover the difference. Finally, at seventy-five she was able to pay off the house."

"We're facing that same thing," Blake said, "Mary lost her dad about six months ago. I don't think he realized he set up his pension to pay out only while he was living, so Mary's mom barely has enough to cover her bills. Fortunately, we've been able to help her with the payments until she can get the house sold. Then she's going to move into that little studio apartment we have off the back of our place. Now that I think about it, all my worrying started about the time Mary's dad died."

A Debt Free Retirement Plan

"My mom's difficulties are part of what sent me looking for a financial advisor. Fortunately, we had toned down our debt when we faced those trials, and we spent the next thirty years working to get debt-free. After we met with Julianne, we started putting extra money into our investments for cars. And right before I retired, we each got a new vehicle. We may need one more in ten years or so, but at least we don't have a payment to worry about now."

"You paid off your house early? Wouldn't you have been better off to keep your low interest mortgage and add to your investments since the return is usually higher?" Blake looked puzzled. "That's what Mary and I have been doing. We still owe more than a hundred thousand on our house."

"That's how many look at it. But Julianne told us that most people feel better when they're out from under the debt when they retire. Since the interest rate on mortgages is usually fixed and the return on investments fluctuates, getting it paid off means we don't have to worry if the market takes a temporary dive. On top of that, it's a matter of cash flow. How much additional cash would you and Donna have if you didn't have to make that payment?"

"Wow, an extra $1500 in our pockets every month would let us breathe easy. Plus, we might be able to travel a bit."

"Yeah, if we were still in our forties, we'd probably want to just keep making that payment, but Julianne made us face our future. She told us we had to think about what we wanted our retirement to look like."

Blake nodded. "I'm going to have to talk to Mary about this, but I'm starting to think we'd be better off pulling back on our 401(k)s during these last twelve months and working to get the house paid off instead. I can feel my stress level go down just thinking about having that extra cash flow."

• • •

Scott was much newer to the sport of pickleball than his friend. It hadn't yet caught on in the small Minnesota town where they both started. Though Blake tried to take it easy on his friend, Scott's competitive nature had him frustrated by the end of their hour.

"I'm going to conquer this game yet," Scott said as they headed to their cars.

"You played better today than our last match," Blake countered. "At least we had fun and got some exercise."

"I think I got extra exercise. You hit that ball all over the place. Maybe if I had played more tennis, I'd have an easier time catching on."

"I hate to take up all your time, but could we meet back here about noon for lunch, so you could give me more advice after we get cleaned up?"

"Definitely. I'll see you then."

If You Have Debt, Make Sure It's Smart Debt

Scott had watched his parents' house mortgage swallow his mother. She became a slave to it. Her financial pain was the final nudge he needed to control his debt. He hated seeing his mother struggle to make ends meet. Though he and his siblings helped as much as they could, since all had children in high school and college at the time, they didn't have much extra to send her way.

It would be difficult for Blake and Mary to pay off their home in a year, but doubling their payment and dropping their 401(k) payments back to the amount their employers matched would get them much closer. While Scott and Donna started minimizing their debt about ten years before retirement, Blake and Mary weren't so fortunate.

Before Blake jumped in the shower, he briefly mentioned to Mary the wisdom of paying the house off early. She was immediately on board, but she reminded him they each still owed three years' worth of payments on their cars, and they'd used credit cards to pay for their last two vacations. Blake knew it was his fault. Mary had tried to talk him into just going away for the weekend every few months, but he felt like he deserved that Caribbean cruise for all his hard work.

Scott and Donna's friends aren't the only ones who find themselves facing the interest rate dilemma on their mortgage. The basic theory of building up your portfolio to get a better return on your investment makes sense, especially if you're forty-five; however, too few think about the peace of mind and potential for adventure that comes with having cash flow. The same rings true with credit card use. The cash and bonus points card companies offer as well as the ease of instant gratification can cripple even those with the highest-paying careers.

One proverb says, "The borrower is servant to the lender."[3] The key to any debt is making it work for you rather than you working to pay off the debt. Some people downsize in retirement to avoid large mortgage payments. Others follow Scott and Donna's example, paying cash for high-ticket items before they retire so they can maintain a good cash flow and truly enjoy the fruits of their labor.

Each person or couple has to decide for themselves how much debt they want to take with them into retirement.

---

[3]   Proverbs 22:7 TLB

However, the earlier we start the conversation, the more equipped we are to make an informed decision. Generally, it's not a good idea to have debt against assets that depreciate like cars, boats, or motorhomes. Armed with knowledge, we can make sure any debt we have as we walk away from our day jobs is smart debt.

LESSON FOUR

I Will Thrive
As I Understand My Financial Picture

Success is neither magical nor mysterious.
Success is the natural consequence
of consistently applying the basic fundamentals.

—*Jim Rohn*

Scott had just given the hostess at the clubhouse his name when Blake walked in the front door. "Right this way, gentlemen."

"So, what's next, Scott?" Blake got the conversation started as they followed her to their seats.

"Next is me deciding what I want for lunch." Scott laughed.

It didn't take long for them to get their drinks and order, and while they waited for food, Blake pressed his friend for more information.

Taking Inventory of Your Assets

After talking to Blake about debt, Scott knew the next part of this conversation would be difficult. Retirement means changing the way we look at assets. Prior to that freedom date, every asset is a number that adds to a person's total equity. Everyone wants to increase their net worth. However, after we leave our career and enter the distribution phase of life, the focus of those assets has to move to cash flow. Net worth means nothing if it can't be liquidated or send cash our way.

Since Blake had struggled a bit with what he'd learned about his mortgage, Scott figured this topic might cause him some stress. But Scott knew without that salary he'd grown accustomed to, Blake would have to live on the income generated from those resources.

"I guess the next lesson we found valuable after we learned to control our debt was understanding how our assets play into retirement. For instance, your house is an asset. Since it's worth a good deal more than you owe on it, it increases your net worth; however, if you have to take an extra fifteen hundred dollars out of your portfolio every month to make the payment, it's going to quickly reduce your rate of return. There are basically three types of assets—those that create cash flow, those that grow (like our investment portfolio), and those that increase our net worth. In retirement, the goal is to have assets that either create cash flow or grow to produce higher cash flow rather than accumulate assets that merely increase our net worth.

"Another reason Donna and I don't stay up nights worrying about the market is because we invested in other assets over the years that are paying off now. We purchased our first outside asset about twenty years ago.

"Every day on my way to the office, I drove by this store that had gone out of business. I watched that For Sale sign in the window fade and fall for two years. One day, I decided to call the number on the sign. It seemed like such a waste. Our little community needed businesses, not empty buildings.

"I discovered the owner hadn't gone out of business. He'd outgrown the location and moved to a bigger city. Because he'd been paying the taxes and utilities for over two years with no revenue, he was anxious to get out from under it. He accepted my first offer, and I started looking for a tenant.

"Within six months, I found a national pharmacy chain that wanted to rent the thirty-five hundred square foot space."

"Oh, yeah. I remember when Town and Country Pharmacy moved into that building on the corner. That was just before Mary and I moved to Arizona."

"Yep, that's the one. At the time, I was focused solely on getting someone in there to cover the mortgage on the building. They made some excellent improvements and signed a ten-year lease. With what they paid in rent, I was able to pay off the loan before the end of their lease and set aside a good amount to take care of building repairs."

Blake looked a bit confused. "But, Scott, what does that have to do with your retirement?"

"Honestly, when I bought it, I thought nothing about retirement. But recently, the pharmacy extended their lease for the second time. Right now, the building is paid off, I have enough set aside for any building repairs that might be needed, and when they signed the current lease—because the cost of real estate is rising—they doubled the amount they'll pay monthly for the next ten years. Even if I put ten percent of their lease payment in an account for building improvements, Donna and I have a retirement income completely independent of the stock market."

"I get it. Did you know Mary and I still own that little house on the south side of town where we lived when we first moved down here? It would be paid off by now, but we renovated when the girls were young. We bought the house we live in now when they were in college. I hadn't even thought about the rent from that place as retirement income. The home improvement loan will be paid off in a few years."

"As long as the cost to maintain it doesn't drag you down. Some people get caught up in the net worth of the asset and forget about the expenses."

Thriving for the Rest of Your Life

The waiter crossed the room with their food as Scott told Blake, "The pharmacy building allows us to keep the distribution from our investments within the sustainable withdrawal rate."

Scott moved his coffee cup out of the way as the tall young man set a plate with his sandwich on it in front of him. "And your soup, sir," the server addressed Blake.

Before he took a bite, Blake stopped Scott. "Wait. Back up. Sustainable what?"

Scott had to finish chewing before he answered. "Sustainable withdrawal rate. Donna and I had never heard of it before either."

Blake waited while Scott took another bite of his sandwich.

"According to Julianne, if we can keep our withdrawal amounts to around 4% of our total portfolio every year, it's possible to maintain our initial investment amount over time—assuming we had around a 50/50 mix of stocks and bonds. Historically, her clients have been able to leave the full amount of their accounts to their children. That means 4% is the current sustainable withdrawal rate. It also means you don't have to guess how long you'll live, because historically, at that rate, accounts have maintained their initial investment."

"But what does that have to do with the building on the corner?"

"Look at it this way. The net lease on that building generates about $60,000 each year. At the 4% withdrawal rate, we would need an additional $1.5 million in our investment accounts to receive the amount of that rent and keep our portfolio sustainable. That's why it's vital we understand our assets and how they add to or rob our cash flow."

"So, would the pension I have coming from this job be considered an asset? I have the option of taking a lump sum at retirement or taking payments. I haven't decided which would be better."

"Definitely an asset. And we'll have to get you hooked up with a financial advisor to answer that question for sure; however, after watching my dad and mom, I know you have to be careful how you fill out the paperwork if you decide to take monthly payments. My dad elected for the larger monthly check, but that meant it ended when he died.

"When you talk to Samantha, she can help you decide whether your pension as an asset would bring you more cash flow as a lump sum or as a monthly income."

• • •

Scott admitted to Blake that before he met Julianne, he paid too much attention to net worth. A mutual friend of theirs had a three-million-dollar home. Unfortunately, just the upkeep on that kind of home stretched him to the limit. On more than one occasion, he had complained to Blake about not being able to retire. At seventy, his net worth outpaced Scott and Blake's combined; however, he lacked a life of thriving because he had little cash flow outside his corporate purchasing management position. Scott once envied this friend because he looked good on paper; however, now that he was experiencing the freedom that understanding assets and cash flow brought, he felt bad for his wealthy friend.

The more Blake talked to Scott, the more his eyes were opened to the places he and Mary needed to improve to have the kind of retirement they talked about. He had started to wonder if he had jumped the gun telling his employer he would train his replacement for a year. They expected him to step down in nine months. Would he and Mary have the cash flow to move into the next phase of their lives and truly thrive? He and Mary needed to meet with Samantha.

I Must Navigate Social Security with Wisdom

Don't wish it was easier, wish you were better.
Don't wish for less problems, wish for more skills.
Don't wish for less challenge, wish for more wisdom.

—*Jim Rohn*

Three weeks after their lunch conversation, Scott and Blake were sitting in a golf cart at the eighth green waiting for the team ahead of them to finish at the tee box. While they waited, Blake brought up another retirement question that had been bothering him. "I know it's none of my business, but you didn't mention getting Social Security when we talked about retirement before."

"That was one of the most confusing things we navigated when we hit sixty-two."

"I thought Social Security would be pretty straightforward. I've paid into it since I had that summer job at a golf course when I was sixteen." Blake thought about all those jobs during his college years as well. "I guess since it's coming from the government, I should have known it would be complicated."

"I'm really not sure how we would have made a decision about Social Security without Julianne's help. There are a variety of scenarios. Each one has advantages, but it depends on individual circumstances. As soon as we finish this round, I'll give you an overview of the four main factors Julianne explained to us."

Word of Wisdom One: Timing

Driving back to the clubhouse after the last green, Scott continued, "So, the Social Security dilemma . . . Julianne told us the number one mistake people make is taking Social Security too early."

"I thought everyone started collecting at age sixty-two or whenever you retired."

"That's one option. But retirees can collect any time after they turn sixty-two, and once you take that first payment, your decision is irrevocable even if your situation changes. Julianne told us retirement is like raising kids. You get one shot at it. No do-overs."

"So, if sixty-two is the earliest, why wouldn't I start collecting then?" Blake sounded confused.

"You could. I have friends who started to collect as soon as they were eligible because they wanted to make sure they got back every penny they put in. Others took the benefit early because they're afraid Social Security won't be around long."

"That sounds logical," Blake said. "I've heard for years that Social Security will be running out soon."

"Julianne explained that experts estimate, at least for our lifetime, Social Security benefits will be fine. And taking benefits out of fear won't maximize our retirement income."

Scott asked Blake the key question as they took their clubs off the cart. "Did you know the amount you receive at age sixty-two isn't your full Social Security benefit?"

"I've heard that it's kind of a sliding scale depending on when you retire, but will I really lose that much if I sign up when I turn sixty-two next year?"

"If you take your Social Security at sixty-two rather than waiting until you reach full retirement age, you could have a reduction of up to thirty-percent."

"Thirty percent?" Blake sounded doubtful. "Are you sure you're not exaggerating?"

"Julianne showed us the numbers. Who would have thought that old proverb would apply to Social Security?"

"Which one is that?"

"An inheritance claimed too soon will not be blessed at the end."[4] Both men laughed.

"Plus," Scott continued, "if you take your benefit at sixty-two and make too much earned income, it could reduce your benefit even more." Scott paused for a moment while he lifted his clubs into the back of his car. "Julianne showed us the list of payouts for our situation over nine years. We discovered that in addition to full retirement age, Social Security has a maximum retirement age. By waiting to delay my social

---

[4]   Proverbs 20:21

security to the maximum age, I will see almost twenty-five percent more in my check each month."

"Wow, that's significant. So, you think I should wait until I reach the maximum benefit age before I start collecting?"

Scott sighed. "I wish it was that simple. Julianne helped me and Donna work out the math to determine how long we should wait. It's different for everyone. Some people definitely benefit by collecting at sixty-two, but there are so many variables. Let me take the cart back, and then I'll meet you in the clubhouse and tell you about them."

Word of Wisdom Two: Taxes

Blake had a table near the window that overlooked the ninth hole when Scott found him.

"I ordered you a burger and a Coke. My treat," Blake said as Scott reached the table. "I appreciate you taking this time to help me get ready for retirement. So, what kind of variables affect us?"

"The taxes we have to pay were one of the big factors in Donna and I originally deciding to push back taking Social Security until we were at least sixty-five."

Blake listened intently as Scott told him that many people don't realize their Social Security benefits can be taxed. Blake admitted he was one.

"Wait, I thought since I contributed to my own Social Security, it wouldn't be taxed once I started to receive it," Blake countered.

Despite Blake's correct logic, it is possible that a large percentage of Social Security benefits may be taxable if a person's total income goes over a certain limit. Because of the different factors they use to determine your combined income, it can become confusing and difficult to control our tax burden.

Scott told Blake, "Julianne advised us to revisit our decision at sixty-five. With our other income, Social Security will push us into a higher tax bracket. Based on current tax law, if we wait until we're sixty-five, we can take advantage of the larger standard deduction."

"So far this sounds like a nightmare."

"Julianne walked us through it right before she retired. Samantha will help us the next time we look at it. But with their help, it wasn't as bad as it sounds."

"So, are taxes the only thing we have to think about?"

Word of Wisdom Three: Spousal Benefits

"I wish. Julianne walked us through two other considerations."

"Since Mary has worked throughout your entire marriage, this one might not affect you, but we found out Donna will probably be able to collect an amount equal to half of my benefit since she hasn't had an outside job since she was thirty."

"How does that work?" Blake was curious even though it wouldn't be a factor for him.

"They call it the spousal benefit. When a couple has a primary breadwinner who contributed more and will receive significantly more than their partner, the spouse who put less in over the years is eligible to claim on the primary breadwinner's account. The amount varies depending on the timing of retirement and how much both people made, but it can be up to fifty percent. Though it was set up in the 1930s, because almost all women were stay-at-home moms, the spousal benefit still helps families who choose to have one parent focus on the kids. In our case, Donna will receive her benefit plus the spousal benefit up to a maximum of fifty-percent of my Social Security benefit at my full retirement age."

Word of Wisdom Four: Survivor Benefits

"I think the thing that will interest you and Mary more is the way the timing of taking our benefit influences our spouses after we're gone."

"You're right. I want to make sure Mary is taken care of if something happens to me," Blake said.

"Actually, doesn't Mary bring in more than you?" Scott smiled.

"Most definitely. She's been the executive assistant to the vice president of her company for ten years. Her paycheck has always outpaced mine. I had to swallow my pride about that a long time ago."

"So, her benefit will be the one you'll want to focus on when you're thinking long term. Regardless of which one of you passes first, her benefit will be the one that lasts the longest.

"In my case, since we chose to have Donna available for the kids, we've opted to wait to take my benefit to give us the largest amount possible regardless of which of us goes first. I don't want Donna to struggle after I'm gone."

"There's so much to know. I'm going to call Samantha when I get home today. We need help navigating all this. Thanks so much, Scott. I really appreciate the time you're taking to walk me through this."

"It's no problem. I still have a couple of lessons we learned from Julianne if you want to hear them."

"I'm in. Maybe you and Donna could come over for lunch after church on Sunday."

"Are you sure Mary won't mind?"

"No worries. I'll cook. We have a phenomenal new grill I'm itching to show off."

"Okay then, we'll see you Sunday."

LESSON SIX

I Can Make Taxes Work for Me Instead of Against Me

Our new Constitution is now established,
everything seems to promise it will be durable;
but, in this world, nothing is certain except death and taxes.

—*Benjamin Franklin*

"**W**e're around back!" Scott and Donna heard Mary's call as they closed the doors on their car. They followed the sidewalk around the light stucco home.

"Hey, guys," Blake called from the grill. "Grab a chair, the steaks are almost done." Mary put the last two glasses on the table and joined them as they waited for their chef to finish.

After enjoying the delicious filets and grilled vegetables, the ladies headed into the living room while Scott and Blake took a dive into one of the more difficult aspects of retirement planning.

How Much Have You Borrowed from Your Rich Uncle

"Let me start with a story someone shared with me years ago," Scott said. "One of my colleagues told me about a man who had an opportunity to buy a small farm just outside of town that would be perfect for his family. Unfortunately, at the time, few banks were willing to give loans because farms in the area were really struggling. He had a relatively wealthy uncle, so he decided to ask him for the $100,000 he needed to buy the farm.

"His uncle was happy to help, but when the man tried to set up a repayment plan and draw up a contract with the interest amount clearly spelled out, the uncle said, 'You don't have to worry about that. We'll work it all out later. I'm doing pretty well now. So, when I need money, we'll work out the details.' Reluctantly the nephew took the money and bought the farm with the interest rate and payment amount hanging over his head.

"For at least a week, the nephew felt the pressure of not knowing how much his uncle expected and what the interest rate should be. My colleague said he heard this story about the same time he and some of the other guys in our office started talking about their retirement plans. A few had chosen to defer taxes on their 401(k)s. Two had advisors that recommended they pay taxes later.

"My colleague said that a light bulb went off as they talked. He had elected tax deferral for his 401(k) as well. The man who had borrowed money from his uncle had been losing sleep because he didn't know how much he was going to end up paying for that $100,000. My colleague realized he never gave his tax-deferred 401(k) a second thought—even though the outcome was basically the same. He had no idea what tax rates would be when he retired, and he couldn't be sure at what age he would end up paying those taxes. Both the man's loan and his deferred taxes lived in the world of the unknown."

Filling Your Buckets

"Wow, I never thought about my tax-deferred investments that way before."

"After I heard this story, Donna and I went to talk to Julianne. She helped us understand if I only made pretax contributions to my 401(k), I would have absolutely no control over the tax rate or payments I would make after I started taking withdrawals. That's when Donna and I decided to invest in non-retirement accounts as well as Roth IRAs. We still put the majority of our money into the pretax accounts, but we knew we wanted to have more flexibility in deciding how much we paid in taxes after we retired."

"So, how does it help having some of your retirement fund in pretax accounts and some in post-tax as well as Roth IRA accounts?" This idea of having control over taxes piqued Blake's curiosity.

"Julianne explained we could put our money in these different tax buckets and then draw from them intentionally. This allows us to manage the tax tables to our advantage."

"I guess I'm going to have to rethink my 401(k)." Blake looked worried.

"Maybe a little. It's not that your 401(k) isn't valuable. I still funded mine after we had the discussion with Julianne. However, by putting some of our contributions in other tax buckets, we've been able to save money now. For instance, when we retired at sixty-two, we had enough set aside that we didn't need to touch our 401(k)s. And as I mentioned, we deferred our Social Security. Our goal was to keep our income in a lower tax bracket until we hit at least sixty-five.

"We also started converting $50,000 a year from our traditional IRAs, an asset that is fully taxable, into a Roth IRA, an asset with no tax on the growth. After ten years with a seven percent return, the $500,000 I had in the traditional IRA—money that would have had tax on the growth—will be worth around $700,000. However, because we converted, the $200,000 in growth will be completely tax-free."

"I have a lot of math to do later this evening," Blake said.

"Wait, before I overwhelm you too much with all this information, there's one more benefit to the Roth IRA bucket. Traditional IRAs have a Required Minimum Distribution. In other words, when you reach a certain age, you have to take out a percentage of the balance from your traditional IRA accounts. Unfortunately, depending on how much you're making in other areas, the small percentage can throw you into a different tax bracket. Julianne wanted to make sure we have as much control as possible on how much we pay in taxes."

"So, how does the Roth help?"

"No RMD."

"No what?"

"RMD—Required Minimum Distribution. You can take what you want when you want it or leave it all for your kids if you don't need it."

"The further into this we get, the more I can see why you found an advisor. I would hate to think about maneuvering through all this myself. I'm really starting to worry that Mary and I waited too long. We wanted to retire next year. She'll be fifty-nine and I'll be sixty-one. A little too young for Social Security, but we figured we'd be all right with pensions and investments."

"Donna and I have talked at length about how blessed we feel that everything fell into place at just the right time. We found Julianne not a moment too soon. Without her stepping in and giving us great advice during those last few years, I would have maxed out my 401(k) contribution every year, and now I would be paying additional taxes. Not to mention the Roth conversions. I wouldn't have thought about doing that in a million years."

About that time Mary walked on the patio with a pitcher. "You two look like you could use some sweet tea."

Donna followed with glasses. "You both look way too serious."

"This is serious stuff." Blake offered a grimace just before he broke into a big smile and took the tea from his wife.

"You two have good timing. We could use a short break." Scott stood and pulled a chair out for Donna then turned to Blake, "Do you have enough brain power left for one more lesson?"

LESSON SEVEN

To Have a Bigger Future, I Must Make Today Matter

Inflation is when you pay fifteen dollars
for the ten–dollar haircut
you used to get for five dollars when you had hair.

—*Sam Ewing*

"To give your brain a bit of a break and still get started on this last lesson, let me tell you about my Aunt Sarah. She taught school in the southeastern part of Minnesota for more than forty years. The teachers in that county had a decent pension plan, and Aunt Sarah had diligently saved during her entire career." Scott turned to Donna. "Do you remember that day we went to visit her about ten years ago? She had just turned eighty-two."

"Yes, what a sweetheart. I felt like she was warning us not to retire. You could see she felt deflated after working so hard for so many years," Donna replied.

Scott continued, "When she turned sixty-five, she decided she deserved to take it easy and have a little fun. She had calculated her expenses down to the penny, so she was confident that between her pension, Social Security, and the small investments she had made over the years, she'd be able to live comfortably.

"However, as she settled into retirement, she began to notice the impact of inflation. First her groceries increased a bit, then her utilities. She didn't think much of it. She knew prices went up, and when costs started rising faster than she'd ever seen in all her years, she assumed it was a temporary increase.

"Gradually, everything she had budgeted for crept higher and higher. She told me, 'Scotty, I thought I would be fine even if I lived well past one hundred, but things have doubled since I retired twenty years ago. Despite the fact everything is more expensive, my pension is fixed, and Social Security increases just haven't kept up.'

"Aunt Sarah found herself dipping into her savings more frequently, and she had to take more from her investments. To make matters worse, healthcare costs soared, eating up a significant portion of her budget. Fortunately, she's always had excellent health, but even the minor things that most seniors need ate away at Aunt Sarah's retirement savings."

Donna picked up the story, "She told us she had planned to travel with several of her friends after retirement. They were all set to go on a cruise when they turned seventy, but she had to cancel because she didn't have enough. When she originally retired, she spoiled her grandchildren with lavish gifts. I could hear the disappointment in her voice when she said she struggled to put a ten dollar bill in each of their birthday cards now."

"That doesn't seem fair," Mary said softly with tears in her eyes.

"Even though she had completely paid off her home before she retired," Scott finished Aunt Sarah's story, "and she gave up her car when she turned eighty, when we talked to her, she could barely make ends meet. She had a modest but comfortable retirement planned. Gross inflation stole it from her."

Prepare for Impact

Blake couldn't see the point. "Honestly Scott, you and I have done fairly well over the years compared to your school teacher aunt who never married. Do we really have to worry about inflation?"

"Not to the extent that we won't be able to buy our grandkids gifts, but every time inflation rises and our income doesn't increase to meet it, we have to live like we took a pay cut. Think about it. Since you and I entered the workforce, we've seen inflation brought on by a number of things—natural disasters, supply and demand, politics, and more. A few times we've even seen it hit double digits. You're right—at least I hope you're right—we'll never be as bad off as Aunt Sarah, but if costs rise by six percent in one year and your pension and Social Security only go up by two, you're going to have to dip into investments which means you won't have as much return on those investments in the following years."

"This has been one of my biggest concerns since Julianne first told us about it." Donna spoke up.

"Really?" You could see the look of surprise on Scott's face. "I had no idea."

"Well, I haven't let it keep me up at night, but we have so little control over inflation. Julianne said inflation is any broad rise in the prices of goods and services across the economy over time. And it eats away the purchasing power for both consumers and businesses.[5] Think about it. The price of gasoline has more than doubled since our kids got their licenses, and food costs have gone up by almost sixty percent.[6]" You could sense Donna's concern for the subject.

Scott picked up the thought. "Real estate has seen a drastic increase. Homes right here in Scottsdale cost nearly four times what they did twenty-five years ago. Do you think our Social Security and pension payments will go up four hundred percent before we turn ninety?"

"Wow! We complain about inflation, but since our employers have kept up with it pretty well, I never thought about how devastating it could be," Blake said.

Mary added her perspective. "And if our companies hadn't given us cost-of-living and merit-based raises, we'd have found new jobs. Blake's company has been great at making sure his compensation is above their competition. But I worked for four other vice presidents before my current boss saw how much work I did for one of his vendors and asked me to join their team. I don't want to have to go out and look for a job after I retire."

"Exactly. Unless you want to supplement your income by working—which will affect the amount you can get from

---

[5] Segal, Troy. *Investopedia.* "What Is Inflation and How Does Inflation Affect Investments?" February 5, 2024. https://www.investopedia.com/ask/answers/what-is-inflation-and-how-should-it-affect-investing/.

[6] *US Inflation Calculator.* "Food Inflation in the United States. Last updated March 12, 2024. https://www.usinflationcalculator.com/inflation/food-inflation-in-the-united-states/.

Social Security until you reach full retirement age—there are no more cost-of-living increases. That's why inflation tends to impact retirees more than the workforce. Every time costs rise, we lose spending power."

Win the Fight

"So, Scott, did Julianne give you any tips on how to win the battle against inflation?" Mary was curious.

"Well," Scott replied, "a few things that help with the inflation fight are lessons that Blake and I have been talking about—keeping retirement debt free, reviewing investments at least annually, and using the tax laws to your advantage. But Donna and I feel like our best defense was finding a financial advisor who knows the ins and outs of the market and keeps an eye on economic trends.

"Julianne told us that during retirement, our everyday decisions will affect our future more than ever. The fact we diversified our portfolio should help. Since inflation has historically averaged around three percent and a diversified portfolio has averaged between six and seven percent, we should be able to keep up with inflation over the long haul."

Donna picked up where Scott left off. "She also recommended keeping no more than an emergency fund in the savings account—you know, enough to pay for a major car repair or an unexpected problem with the house that insurance won't cover. Since interest rates on savings accounts tend to be very low, we're much better off to have those funds in our portfolio if we want that money to keep up with inflation."

"Inflation can be one of the most difficult parts of retirement because it's so unpredictable," Scott continued. "But after talking to Julianne, I feel like we've done everything possible to brace for it."

Mary spoke up. "We have a video appointment with Samantha next Wednesday. It's time we made sure we're prepared to retire."

Blake stood. "Anyone up for a game of cards before you guys head home?"

"Sounds good," Scott answered.

"I'll be right back with cards and dessert. Then Mary and I will show you how it's done."

One Year Later

Blessed are those who find wisdom,
those who gain understanding

—Proverbs 3:13 (NIV)

Scott smiled and waved as he entered the gated community where he and Donna had lived for nearly three years now. He and the gatekeeper had hit it off the first time they visited The Legends. The small neighborhood was home to several Minnesota transplants, including the man who checked IDs of those who didn't have key cards to enter.

Bicycles had the right-of-way the final half mile to the house, but the slow pace allowed him to enjoy the meticulously landscaped lawns and wave at the neighbors sitting on their front porches.

He and Donna had been doubly blessed to find this house on Crenshaw Drive. Not only did it allow them to entertain their entire family with ample space, the view of the sixth green with a backdrop of saguaro cactuses growing on the jagged hills added immense peace to their lives.

They had purchased the home two winters before they moved in, and the fact it needed major updates had saved them enough to do the work and keep the price in their spending range. Plus, Donna loved the freedom to oversee the interior design as they remodeled during that year before they retired.

Scott hadn't even gotten out of his car when Donna pulled into the driveway after golfing with the women's league.

"Did you have a good lunch with Blake?" Donna asked.

"As always. I miss golfing with him on Thursdays."

"He'll be back on the league in no time. He's only going to consult for two years, right?"

The Best Laid Plans

After Blake and Mary's video call with Samantha, they decided to work two years longer than originally planned so they could get the house paid off and add significantly to their investments. Since Blake had already made arrangements to turn the reigns of the purchasing department to the company's new hire, he started freelance consulting. He was surprised how many companies wanted someone with his experience to come in for a couple of months to help get their procurement departments back on track. And he could make almost twice as much as a consultant.

Benjamin Franklin said, "If you fail to plan, you are planning to fail." Though Blake and Mary had a plan, they had also made many erroneous assumptions which can just as easily undermine success. Fortunately, a two-year detour would put them back on their path to freedom.

A Bigger Future

"I'm glad we met Julianne ten years before we wanted to retire," Donna told Scott. "Otherwise, we might have been in the same boat as Blake and Mary—not nearly as prepared as we thought."

Scott and Donna poured glasses of iced tea before they moved out onto the patio. In just a couple months, they'd be back in Minnesota for the summer. If you asked which home they preferred, they'd have a difficult time deciding. They loved spending time with their children and grandchildren, and they felt fortunate to have such a beautiful place full of good friends to stay out of the cold.

The comfortable silence as they sat near the pool gave them an opportunity to consider their blessings—three independent children, each with careers they loved, seven grandchildren excelling in school and having fun in sports and extracurriculars, as well as two beautiful homes to experience life in. Donna enjoyed her creative arts classes, book clubs, and pickleball and golf leagues. In addition to Thursdays on the course, Scott discovered a passion for working with his hands doing minor repairs around the house—especially after all those years of sitting behind a desk.

Scott also spent the quiet time thinking about his lunch conversation with Blake.

• • •

"So, what's your favorite thing about retirement," Blake had asked him.

"I think it's the freedom to live out a Dan Sullivan quote I heard when I was working. It's rattled around in my head for more than five years, and now I can follow it more than ever before."

"So, what's the quote?"

"'Always make your future bigger than your past,'"[7] Scott replied. "I've achieved a lot in my life, but I don't want to live on the coattails of my past accomplishments. Staying focused on all I've done, even when I've been charitable, will get boring quickly. I love the thought of working to make a bigger future. Focusing on making the next ninety days bigger than the last ninety makes life adventurous. It forces me to consider where I want to be in two years or five, and the challenge makes me look forward to getting up in the morning."

"I think the best bigger future would be bigger bank accounts." Blake laughed as he shared.

"That's where you and I have different mindsets, Blake. I just can't get excited about accumulating money for the sake of having money. Even when I was working, I felt like the money needed to serve a better purpose. Now, more than ever, I want to use my finances to better myself and help others. I never want to stop growing."

Scott went on. "I guess that's my favorite thing about retirement. I feel like I have more time to create opportunities for growth. For the past two summers, Donna and I have spent more intentional time with our kids and grandkids. And those plane tickets for the older grandchildren—that's money invested in growing relationships.

"I have more time for golf and pickleball, so I can improve my health. And I love the extra opportunities to

---

[7]   Dan Sullivan

grow spiritually—I've learned so much in that mid-week men's study group.

"Do you remember when Donna and I went to Tuscany last winter? We stayed at Villa Delia and indulged in their culinary school package. Now, we take turns cooking gourmet meals, and we try something new every week."

"Hearing you talk, I feel like I'm drifting through life. I guess I thought retirement meant I was done." Blake looked deflated.

"Most of the population takes that approach to their retirement years. But the thought of living that way bores me."

"So, what's next for you, then? From the sounds of it, you're not finished."

It was Scott's turn to laugh. "You're right. Donna and I signed up for two mission trips through the church. One this winter from down here, and one next fall out of Minnesota. Plus, I've been looking into partnering with SCORE™."

"What's SCORE?"

"It's a non-profit that mentors entrepreneurs to help them get their businesses off the ground. I've already been talking to some of the successful small business owners in our area. We should have a good team of volunteers ready to go within the next couple of months."

"After setting up my own consulting business this summer, I think I might like to help with that after I retire. Even though I could handle the purchasing part of this consulting gig with my eyes closed, I had quite a few things to learn about being my own boss."

"I'll add you to my database. See, you've already started your list of 'ways to make your future bigger.'"

Back in Minnesota

Ethan spent a few days of his vacation at home before heading to the beach with his friends for Memorial Day weekend. He'd been at his new job for almost a year and loved it. Scott and Donna felt blessed that their oldest grandson would stop in to visit when he had such limited time at home.

Donna set pieces of pie in front of the two men as Ethan continued to tell them about his new job. "I talked with Samantha, Grandpap. She told me to go ahead and put the matching amount in the 401(k) at work. Did you know if you skip the match, it's like throwing money away every payday?"

Scott and Donna smiled at each other with a bit of pride.

Ethan continued. "She also helped me set up a Roth IRA and an investment portfolio. Because I'm renting an apartment with two guys I graduated with, I can put almost half of my paycheck into savings and retirement, and still have plenty to pay the bills and have a little fun on the weekend."

"I'm so glad you got started so young, Ethan," Donna said. "With what you saved during high school and college and everything you're adding to your savings now, I'll bet you'll be able to pay cash for your next car. Scott, can you imagine how much we could have saved if we'd been able to avoid interest on all our vehicles?"

"How many car loans have we had since we got married?" The older couple laughed.

As they finished their pie, Ethan told Scott and Donna about his next project. He'd been invited to be on the team that would travel to evaluate the next build. When Scott asked if there was a girl in the picture yet, the young man blushed a bit and shared news he hadn't even told his parents—he'd been dating a girl for about three months, and it seemed kind of serious. If everything went well, they'd get to meet her at Thanksgiving.

Though their visit was brief, Scott and Donna appreciated every moment.

• • •

About a week later, a delivery arrived on the front porch.

"What did you order now?" Scott teased Donna.

"It wasn't me this time. Must be something you forgot you ordered."

Scott cut the tape, opened the box, and lifted out a sculpture that looked like the Scottsdale skyline. He found a note at the bottom of the box.

Dear Scott,

Thanks so much for taking time to help me see how much I needed to talk to your financial advisor. Mary and I can't believe how wrong we were about what we thought we knew about retirement. I especially appreciate you sharing your heart about making your future bigger. My outlook was so small, but Mary and I have big plans now. The church is planning a mission trip that will leave the summer after we retire. It seems far off now, but time passes so quickly—especially since I'm trying to learn Spanish so I'll be more useful when we go. Mary and I hope that every time you and Donna look at this sculpture, you'll remember you have people who care about you in your Arizona home.

Can't wait to see you in November,

Blake and Mary

PART THREE

Pathways

What are YOU trying to accomplish?
Do you have Whos in your life that give you the perspectives,
resources, and ability to go beyond what you could do alone?
Or are you keeping your goals so small
to make them easier to accomplish on your own?

—*Dan Sullivan*

Next Steps

Action is what converts
human dreams into significance.

—*John Maxwell*

By now, perhaps you're thinking you need to find your own Julianne—Scott and Donna's fictional financial advisor. Fortunately, her wisdom represents a composite of advice our firm and others who focus on retirement planning have given to clients over the past three decades. Though we've been doing this for more than thirty-five years, much has changed in the financial world since we started—another reason someone like Julianne can be extremely helpful. Wisdom from your parents might have expired. Fluctuating laws, age requirements, and individual employer policies mean that the way your brother took disbursements five years ago may not be applicable to you. Finding someone who specializes in staying knowledgeable in the financial aspects of life can be invaluable.

Life gives each of us three common financial hurdles to cross. While you may encounter extras, nearly everyone faces the challenges of buying and maintaining a home, funding college for their children, and retirement. Likewise, most think nothing of contacting a realtor and a banker when they're ready to buy their home. And finding an investment advisor for the kids' college funds seems like a no-brainer. Too often, though, people think retirement is cut and dry, so they attempt to maneuver it on their own. Why would we do this when expert advice and assistance is as close as an email or a phone call?

Find Meaning and Purpose

Not long ago, I decided I wanted to help retirees do more than merely survive through retirement. We want something bigger than an Aunt Sarah life. Right? It's more than just crunching numbers to give you some assurance you won't run out of money before you run out of breath. Thriving after retirement goes beyond taking cruises and being able to fish the biggest lakes in the nation. These seven lessons play a vital part in living well after sixty; however, none of them matter if you don't use your freedom to live with even greater purpose and meaning.

Most of us have twenty to thirty productive years left when we give up our day jobs. I bet that's longer than some of the positions you held. By learning the seven lessons Scott shared with Blake, we can set ourselves up for a few successful decades. I had one client break their retirement years into three categories—their go-go years from age sixty to seventy-five, their slow-go years from age seventy-five through eighty-five, and their no-go years to describe those days of lost mobility. The goal is to have enough to fund your go-go phase, yet still carry you in your no-go phase.

By following these lessons, we can achieve financial security that allows us to turn our passion into power and our aspirations into achievements. It's vital to dream big. Do you want to travel, buy a home in the sun, or renovate your home?

Many enjoy using the fruit of their wise planning as an opportunity to be philanthropic. Who do you want to help? Have you been hoping to go to Honduras or Haiti to build houses or feed children? Maybe Habitat for Humanity or some other service organization appeals to you. Or perhaps you'd simply like to be able to mow lawns for your neighbors in their no-go years. No goal is too big or too small as long as you've made a plan to fund your vision.

I encourage you to find an advisor who will review your bucket list and financial plan to ensure you have appropriate short-term and long-term finances available during the various stages of your retirement journey. And remember, it's never too early to start the discussion.

What Do I Look for in a Financial Advisor?

Julianne set the bar high in the realm of financial advisors, but you really shouldn't settle for any less. To make sure your accumulation years will take you through your distribution years, you need to find someone, or a group of professionals, who will take you from investment management, tax and income strategies, strategic philanthropy, and retirement planning to estate planning.

There are a variety of designations for financial planners—from Certified Financial Planners (CFP®) and

Certified Investment Management Analysts (CIMA®) to Certified Public Accountants (CPA®), Enrolled Agents (EA®), and everything in between. The alphabet soup of designations can be intimidating. CFPs and CIMAs have the broadest skillsets. They can offer advice on every area of your financial journey and are held to the highest ethical standards. On the other end of the spectrum, CPAs, EAs, and others have niche specialties—taxes, retirement, IRS regulations and more.

Whichever you choose, it's important to find someone with experience who shares your investment philosophy as well as your communication style. The perfect financial advisor should encourage questions and be responsive to your inquiries.

Additionally, a great advisor provides behavior coaching. Sometimes we need the voice of reason when we're being overly cautious or too willing to take a chance. The advice of someone with an outside perspective can help us make better decisions in the moment that will transform the potential of our future.

As you begin to maneuver the journey of retirement planning, look for the online tools many firms offer to get started. Often, you can get a preview of how your contributions could affect your goal and better understand how comfortable you are with risk. While some folks are willing to face the uncertainty of more volatile investments with the chance of a higher rate of return, others prefer to play it safe. The most important step you'll take as you prepare for your future is to find someone who will help you embrace the next chapter of your life with purpose, wealth, and confidence. As the well-informed Scotts of the world will tell you, with the right retirement plan in place, it is possible to *Retire and Thrive*.

Further Resources

If you relate to Blake in his quest to put his household finances in order and prepare for the future, we invite you to explore RetireAndThrive.net to find a number of resources to enhance your post-career journey! From practical retirement to-do lists, interactive calculators, and insightful videos, you'll find information to help you embark on your new adventure. Whether you're pondering the right time to take social security, looking at pension choices, or debating the merits of Roth IRA conversions, RetireAndThrive.net is your ultimate companion for navigating the complexities of retirement.

Key Takeaways

Part One: Parable

1. Whatever your age as you read this, begin today to prepare for retirement.
2. Children change your investment strategy.
3. Life will throw things your way you can't control.

Part Two: Paradigm

Lesson One: I Can Enjoy the Fruits of My Labor

1. Use your empty nest years as accumulation years.
2. Find a financial advisor.
3. Give yourself permission to enjoy retirement.

Lesson Two: To Reap the Rewards, I Must Review My Investments

1. Choose an advisor who schedules regular portfolio reviews.

2. Create long- and short-term financial goals.

3. Owning stocks makes you a business owner.

Lesson Three: I Only Have Freedom When My Cash Flows Freely

1. Debt in retirement can hinder cash flow.

2. If you don't control your debt, it will control you.

3. Taking funds from your portfolio to cover debt will reduce your long-term return.

Lesson Four: I Will Thrive As I Understand My Financial Picture

1. Retirement means a change in the way we view assets.

2. We have three types of assets—those that grow, those that increase cash flow, and those that increase net worth.

3. In retirement, we need assets to increase cash flow.

Lesson Five: I Must Navigate Social Security with Wisdom

1. With Social Security, timing is everything.

2. Social Security can greatly impact taxes.

3. We need to time our Social Security to optimize spousal and survivor benefits.

Lesson Six: I Can Make Taxes Work for Me Instead of Against Me?

1. If you borrowed from your rich uncle you would want to know the rate and payment. Treat taxes the same way.

2. You may not want your entire retirement fund in a tax-deferred 401(k).

3. Don't let the Required Minimum Distribution throw you into a higher tax bracket.

Lesson Seven: To Have a Bigger Future, I Must Make Today Matter

1. Social Security and pension benefits don't always grow at the same rate as inflation.

2. Inflation eats away your purchasing power.

3. Diversification can help you win the fight against inflation.

Part Three: Pathways

1. Finding someone who specializes in staying knowledgeable in the financial aspects of life can be invaluable.

2. Following these lessons can help us achieve financial security that allows us to turn our passion into power and our aspirations into achievements.

3. It's important to find a financial advisor with experience who also shares your investment philosophy as well as your communication style.

About the Author

Dan Langworthy is the Founder of Fortress Financial Group and a Financial Advisor with over 35 years of experience in the financial services industry. His professional credentials include certification by the Investments & Wealth Institute as a Certified Investment Manager Analyst (CIMA®) and a Certified Private Wealth Advisor (CPWA®).

Dan is a frequent keynote speaker and a highly sought-after expert who is often interviewed about personal finance management, investment strategies, retirement planning, and the impact of global events on personal finance.

Fortress Financial Group, LLC ("Fortress") is a registered investment advisor. Advisory services are only offered to clients or prospective clients where Fortress and its representatives are properly licensed or exempt from licensure.

The information provided is for educational and informational purposes only and does not constitute investment advice and it should not be relied on as such. It should not be considered a solicitation to buy or an offer to sell a security. It does not take into account any investor's particular investment objectives, strategies, tax status or investment horizon. You should consult your attorney or tax advisor.

No investment strategy or risk management technique can guarantee returns or eliminate risk in any market environment.

All investments include a risk of loss that clients should be prepared to bear. The principal risks of Fortress' strategies are disclosed in the publicly available Form ADV Part 2A.

Diversification does not ensure a profit or guarantee against loss.

Generally, among asset classes, stocks are more volatile than bonds or short-term instruments. Government bonds and corporate bonds have more moderate short-term price fluctuations than stocks, but provide lower potential long-term returns. U.S. Treasury Bills maintain a stable value if held to maturity, but returns are generally only slightly above the inflation rate.

ARE YOU PREPARED TO

RETIRE AND THRIVE?

Discover Your

RETIREMENT READINESS SCORE™

Scan the QR code or Visit:
RetireAndThrive.net/Readiness

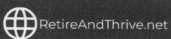

THIS BOOK IS PROTECTED INTELLECTUAL PROPERTY

The author of this book values Intellectual Property. The book you just read is protected by Easy IP®, a proprietary process, which integrates blockchain technology giving Intellectual Property "Global Protection." By creating a "Time-Stamped" smart contract that can never be tampered with or changed, we establish "First Use" that tracks back to the author.

Easy IP® functions much like a Pre-Patent™ since it provides an immutable "First Use" of the Intellectual Property. This is achieved through our proprietary process of leveraging blockchain technology and smart contracts. As a result, proving "First Use" is simple through a global and verifiable smart contract. By protecting intellectual property with blockchain technology and smart contracts, we establish a "First to File" event.

Protected By Easy IP®

LEARN MORE AT EASYIP.TODAY